THE GREAT AMERICAN DUST BOWL

TO BETH & THOM

WWW.HMHCO.COM

PHOTOS: P. 78 NATIONAL OCEANIC AND ATMOSPHERIC ADMINISTRATION/ DEPARTMENT OF COMMERCE; P. 80 MARK J. REBILAS / US PRESSWIRE

THE TEXT OF THIS BOOK IS SET IN CC TIM SALE BRUSH.
THE ILLUSTRATIONS ARE PEN & INK WITH DIGITAL PAINT.

ISBN 978-0-547-81550-3
MANUFACTURED IN USA
PHX 10 9 8 7 6 5 4 3
4500510441

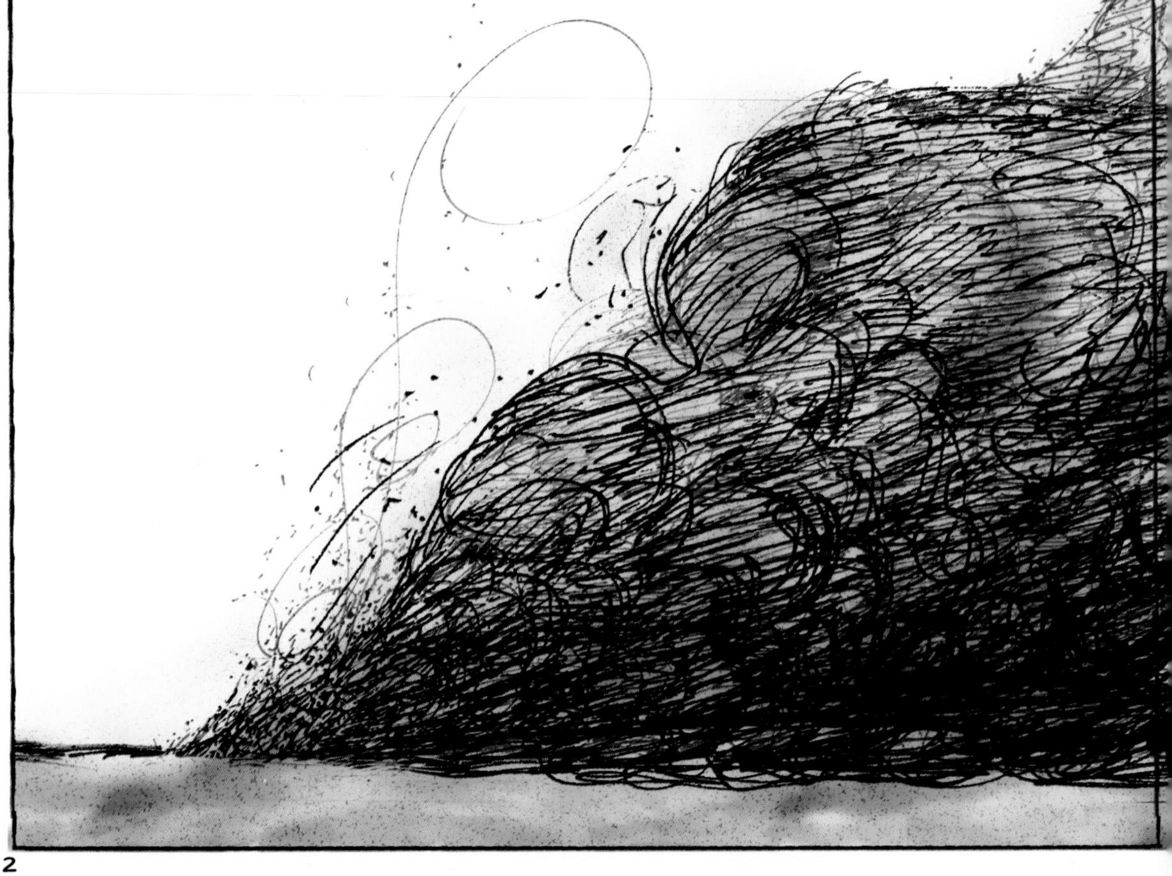

THE GREAT AMERICAN DUST BOWL

WRITTEN & ILLUSTRATED BY
DON BROWN

HOUGHTON MIFFLIN

HOUGHTON MIFFLIN HARCOURT

BOSTON NEW YORK   2013

A SPECK OF DUST IS A TINY THING.
FIVE OF THEM COULD FIT ON THE PERIOD
AT THE END OF THIS SENTENCE.

OH MY GOD!
HERE IT COMES!

On a clear, warm Sunday, April 14, 1935, a wild wind whipped up billions upon billions of specks of dust to form a savage storm on America's plains. Panicked birds and rabbits fled. The temperature plummeted fifty degrees. Electricity coursed through the air. Frightened people raced to the nearest shelter.

But the story of the Black Sunday monster started much, much earlier . . .

SIXTY TO ONE HUNDRED MILLION YEARS AGO, THE ROCKY MOUNTAINS IN NORTH AMERICA WERE BORN. IMMENSE SECTIONS OF THE EARTH'S SURFACE CALLED PLATES, SLOWLY RIDING CURRENTS OF HOT, SOFT ROCK SWIMMING BENEATH THEM, MET.

Tectonic Plates

ONE PLATE SLID BENEATH THE OTHER IN A PROCESS CALLED SUBDUCTION.

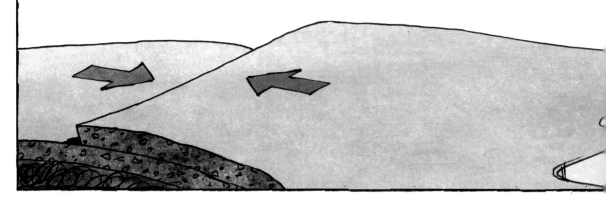

THE LOWER PLATE, ALONG WITH GREAT FORCES WITHIN THE EARTH, LIFTED THE UPPER PLATE.

THE ROCKIES WERE BORN

TO THE EAST OF THE NEW MOUNTAINS LAY A HUGE SHALLOW SEA. IN TIME, IT DRIED UP, AND ITS FLAT, FLAT SEA FLOOR BECAME A FLAT, FLAT PLAIN. THE PLAIN, WHICH STRETCHES EASTWARD TO THE MISSISSIPPI RIVER, IS ONE OF THE MOST LEVEL PLACES ON EARTH.

AND THE PLAIN BEHIND IT ROSE THOUSANDS OF FEET ABOVE SEA LEVEL.

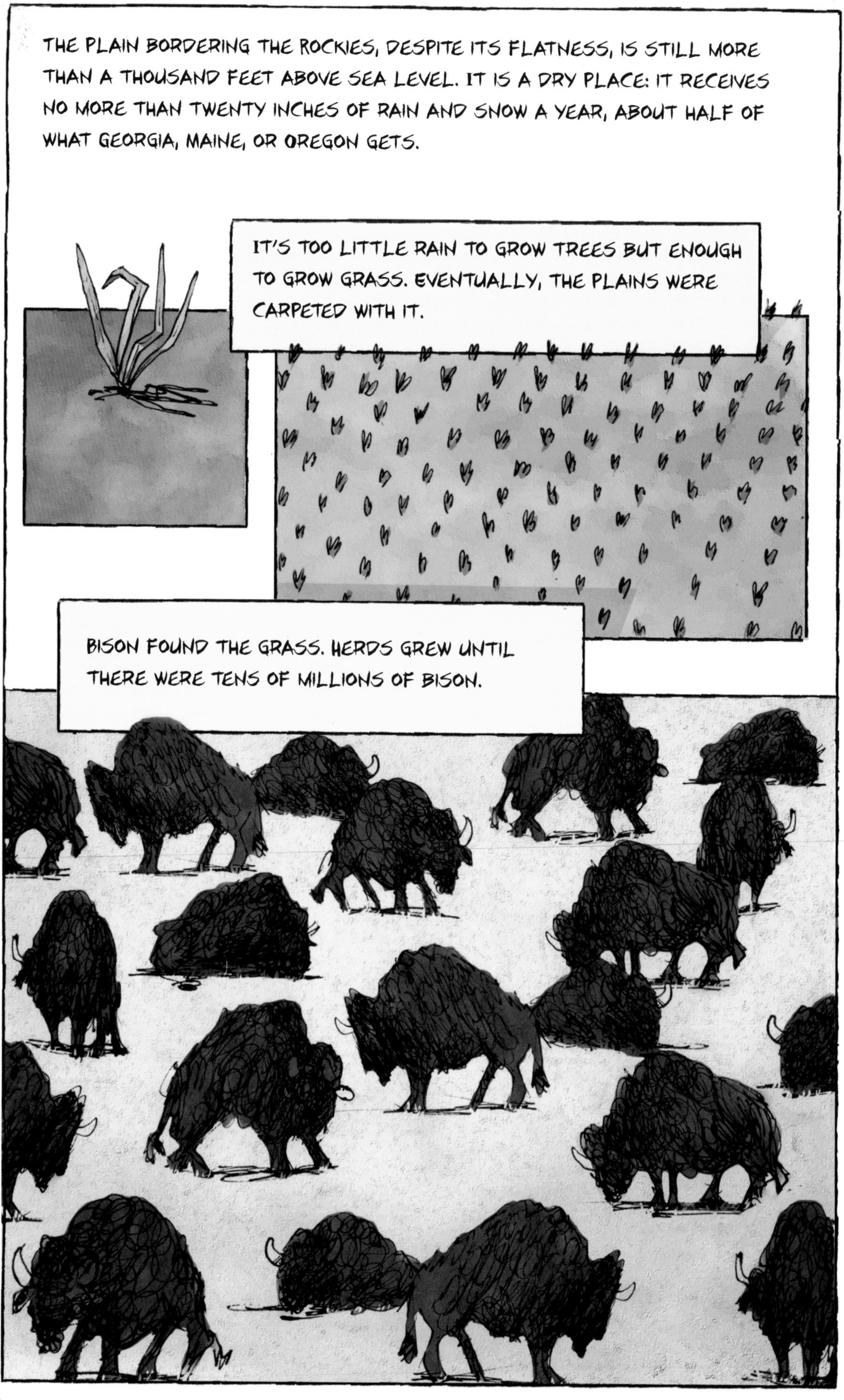
THE PLAIN BORDERING THE ROCKIES, DESPITE ITS FLATNESS, IS STILL MORE THAN A THOUSAND FEET ABOVE SEA LEVEL. IT IS A DRY PLACE: IT RECEIVES NO MORE THAN TWENTY INCHES OF RAIN AND SNOW A YEAR, ABOUT HALF OF WHAT GEORGIA, MAINE, OR OREGON GETS.
IT'S TOO LITTLE RAIN TO GROW TREES BUT ENOUGH TO GROW GRASS. EVENTUALLY, THE PLAINS WERE CARPETED WITH IT.
BISON FOUND THE GRASS. HERDS GREW UNTIL THERE WERE TENS OF MILLIONS OF BISON.

AMERICAN INDIANS FOUND THE BISON AND MADE THEM THE CENTER OF THEIR CULTURE, USING THEM FOR FOOD, CLOTHING, AND SHELTER. THE INDIANS, THE BUFFALO, THE LAND, AND THE WEATHER EXISTED IN A BALANCE FOR MORE THAN A THOUSAND YEARS.

PIONEERS FROM THE SETTLED, EASTERN UNITED STATES CAME TO THE PLAINS IN THE NINETEENTH CENTURY. BY 1876, THEY HAD PUSHED THE INDIANS INTO RESERVATIONS AND SLAUGHTERED MILLIONS OF BISON. RANCHERS AND CATTLE REPLACED THE INDIANS AND BUFFALO.

RANCHERS WERE SURE THAT THE "IMMENSITY OF GRASS" THAT HAD SUPPORTED THE BISON WOULD SUSTAIN CATTLE. IN THE SOUTHERN PLAINS, NEARLY EIGHT HUNDRED MILES OF BARBED-WIRE FENCE PENNED IN ABOUT 150,000 HEAD OF CATTLE.

BUT CATTLE LACKED THE STURDINESS OF BISON, AND THE SUMMER HEAT AND WINTER BLIZZARDS WIPED THEM OUT.

RICHES IN THE SOIL! PROSPERITY IN THE AIR! PROGRESS EVERYWHERE!

THE RANCHERS' HARD LUCK DIDN'T DARKEN THEIR SALES PITCH WHEN THEY DECIDED TO UNLOAD THE LAND: FARMERS BOUGHT, SOMEHOW OVERLOOKING THAT THE PLEDGES OF WEALTH CAME FROM THE FAILED RANCHERS.

FROM SOD HOUSES, CRUDE SHACKS, AND DUGOUT EARTHEN HOMES, FARMERS WORKED THE LAND.

DESPITE THEIR SWEAT AND HIGH HOPES, THE FARMERS WERE ONLY ABLE
TO SCRATCH OUT A MEAGER LIVELIHOOD FROM THE TOUGH LAND AND HARD
WEATHER . . . THEN INTERNATIONAL TRAGEDY DELIVERED RICHES.

THE BLOODY FIRST WORLD WAR OF 1914 TO 1918 WRECKED MUCH OF EUROPE, INCLUDING ITS FARMING.

MANY PEOPLE HAD A TERRIBLE TIME GETTING FOOD.

A HUNGRY WORLD BECAME AN EAGER MARKET, AND THE PRICE OF WHEAT JUMPED.

SEEING THE PROFIT IN IT, FARMERS ON THE SOUTHERN PLAINS UPTURNED MILLIONS OF ACRES OF GRASSLAND AND SOWED THE PRICEY GRAIN.

PLOWING ALL THOSE ACRES WAS MADE EASIER AS THE FARMERS TRADED THEIR HORSES FOR TRACTORS. A TRACTOR TOOK THREE HOURS TO DO THE WORK FOR WHICH A TEAM OF HORSES NEEDED FIFTY-EIGHT HOURS. SUDDENLY FARMERS ENJOYED A BOUNTY THAT HAD ESCAPED EARLIER. ONE FROM KANSAS CLAIMED A YEAR'S PROFIT OF $75,000, MORE MONEY THAN THE PRESIDENT IN WASHINGTON MADE.

THEN THE WAR ENDED. LIFE, AND FARMING, RETURNED TO NORMAL FOR MUCH OF THE WORLD, AND THE DEMAND FOR AMERICAN FOOD FELL. WHERE ONCE A BUSHEL OF WHEAT EARNED A FARMER TWO DOLLARS, IT NOW FETCHED ONE. SEEING THEIR IN-COME CUT IN HALF, THE FARMERS TRIED TO CORRECT THE LOSS BY GROWING TWICE AS MUCH. MORE SOD WAS BROKEN AND PLANTED IN WHEAT. BUT EVENTUALLY THE ADDITIONAL GRAIN COULDN'T FIND ENOUGH BUYERS, AND PRICES COLLAPSED.

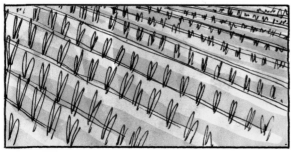

IT WAS LIKE SOMEBODY JUST SHUT THE DOOR ON OUR LIVES.

AS WHEAT'S VALUE CRASHED, THE GREAT DEPRESSION STRUCK THE AMERICAN ECONOMY. IN 1929, NEARLY A QUARTER OF THE COUNTRY WAS WITHOUT JOBS AND MONEY. GRAIN SILOS BURST WITH UNWANTED WHEAT, AND A BUSHEL DROPPED TO 34¢, AND THEN TO 24¢—LESS THAN IT HAD COST THE FARMER TO PLANT AND HARVEST IT. SOUTHERN PLAINS GROWERS SLIPPED INTO POVERTY WITH THE REST OF THE NATION.

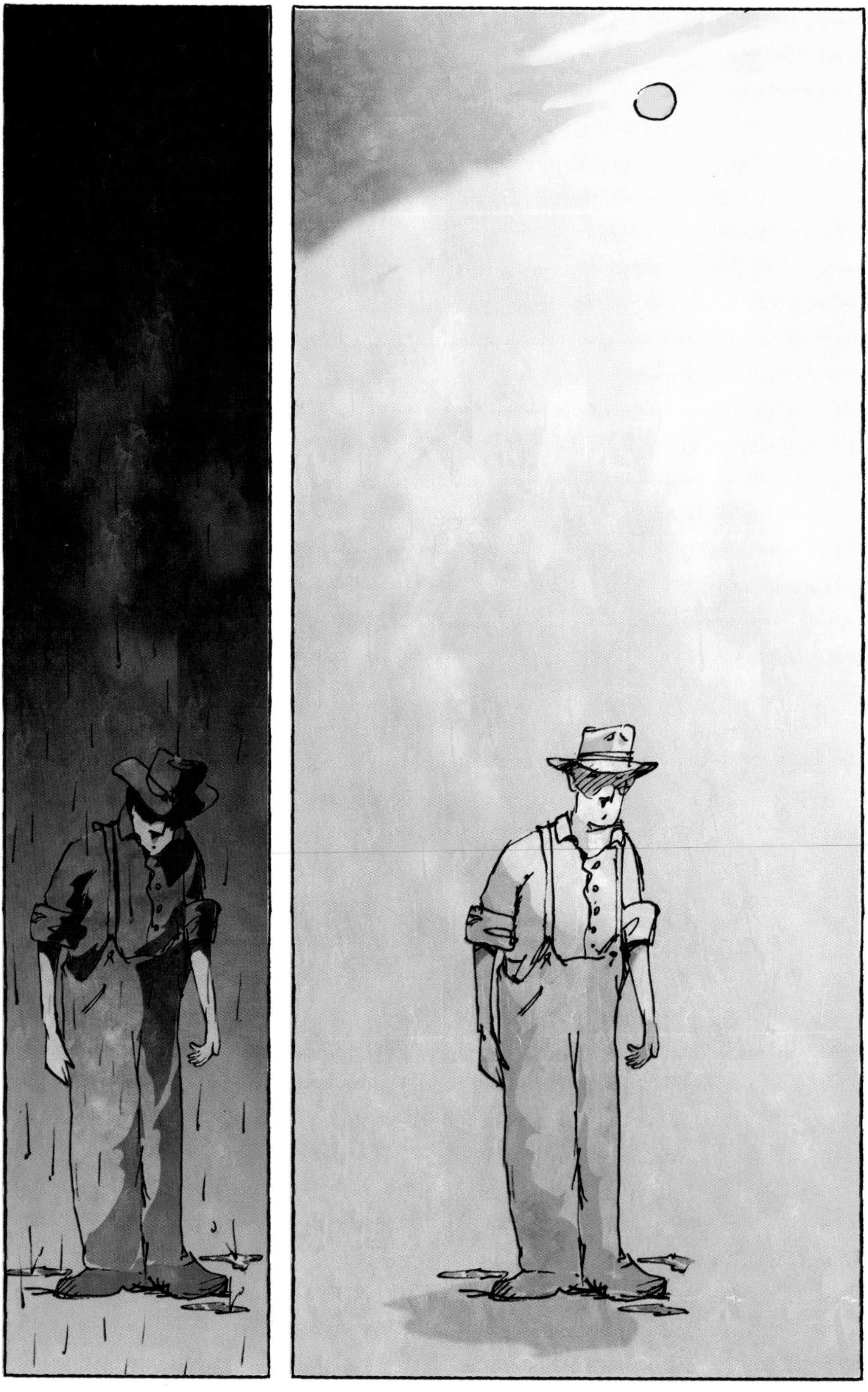

IN 1931, THE RAINS STOPPED AND THE MISERY
OF THE SOUTHERN PLAINS DEEPENED.

THE DROUGHT TORTURED THE LAND, EVAPORATING THE MOISTURE IN THE SOIL. YOU COULD HAVE DUG A THREE-FOOT HOLE AND NOT FOUND A DROP OF WATER. NEITHER GRASS NOR WHEAT COULD HOLD THE DRY, PULVERIZED EARTH TOGETHER. WHEN THE WIND BLEW, DUST STORMS FOLLOWED.

PEOPLE SURVIVED ON THE SMALL AMOUNT OF WATER THEY COULD PUMP FROM THE GROUND.

IN JANUARY 1932, WIND BLEW DIRT TEN THOUSAND FEET INTO THE AIR, NEARLY TWENTY TIMES HIGHER THAN THE WASHINGTON MONUMENT. THE SKY TURNED BROWNISH GRAY. SIXTY-MILE-PER-HOUR, DIRT-FILLED WINDS LASHED TEXAS, OKLAHOMA, AND KANSAS. PEOPLE CALLED IT "AWE-INSPIRING."

FOURTEEN MORE DUSTERS—DUST STORMS—OCCURRED THAT YEAR ALONE. CLOUDS OF DUST WOULD BOIL TO THE HEAVENS, SOMETIMES WITH SPOOKY SILENCE AND OTHER TIMES ACCOMPANYING THE FLASH AND ROAR OF A RAINLESS THUNDERSTORM.

A TERRIBLE DUST STORM CAME IN. THE WAY THE SUN WAS SHINING, IT LOOKED LIKE FIRE, AND I THOUGHT TO MYSELF, *SURELY THIS IS THE END OF THE WORLD.*

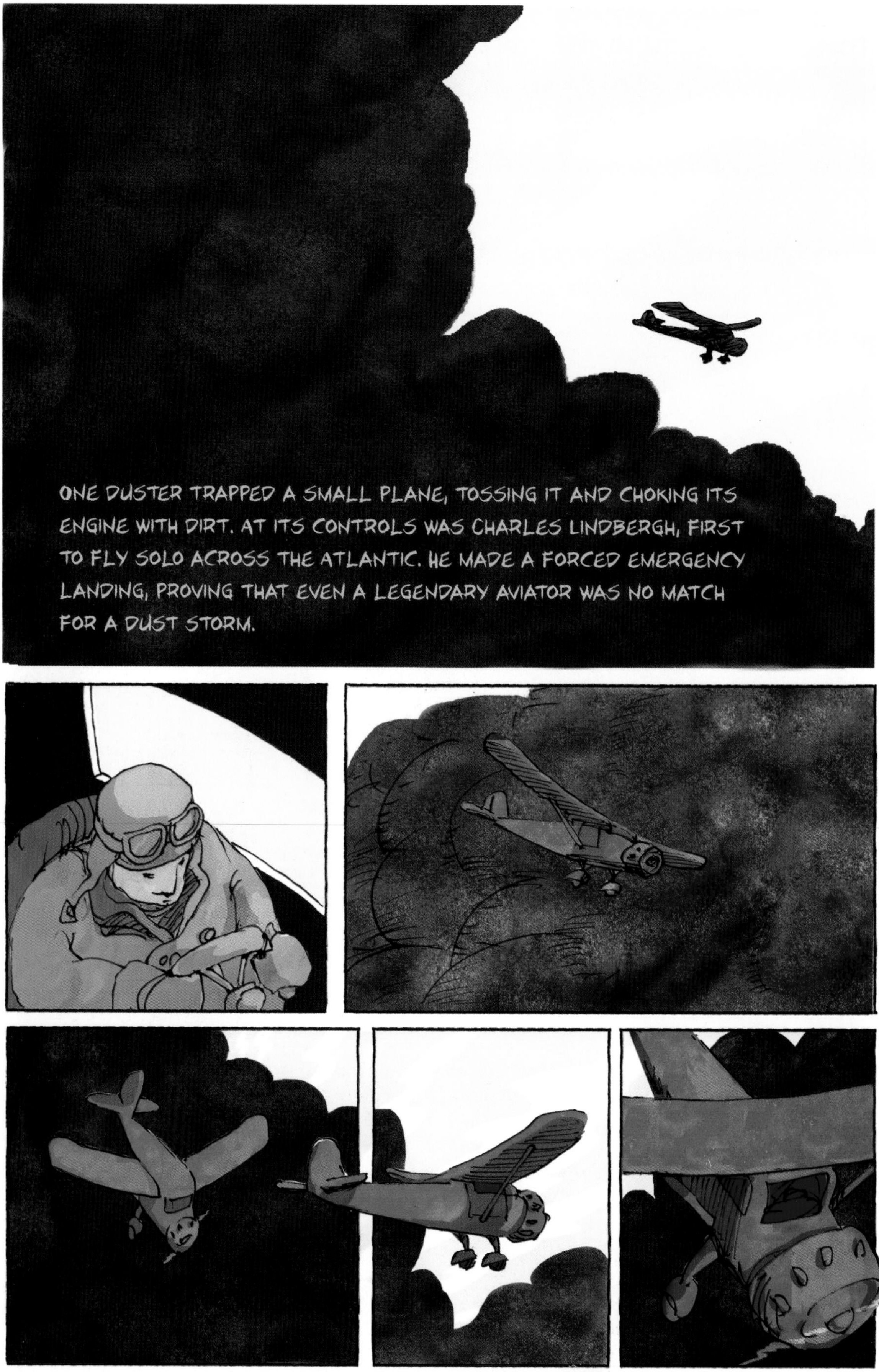
ONE DUSTER TRAPPED A SMALL PLANE, TOSSING IT AND CHOKING ITS ENGINE WITH DIRT. AT ITS CONTROLS WAS CHARLES LINDBERGH, FIRST TO FLY SOLO ACROSS THE ATLANTIC. HE MADE A FORCED EMERGENCY LANDING, PROVING THAT EVEN A LEGENDARY AVIATOR WAS NO MATCH FOR A DUST STORM.

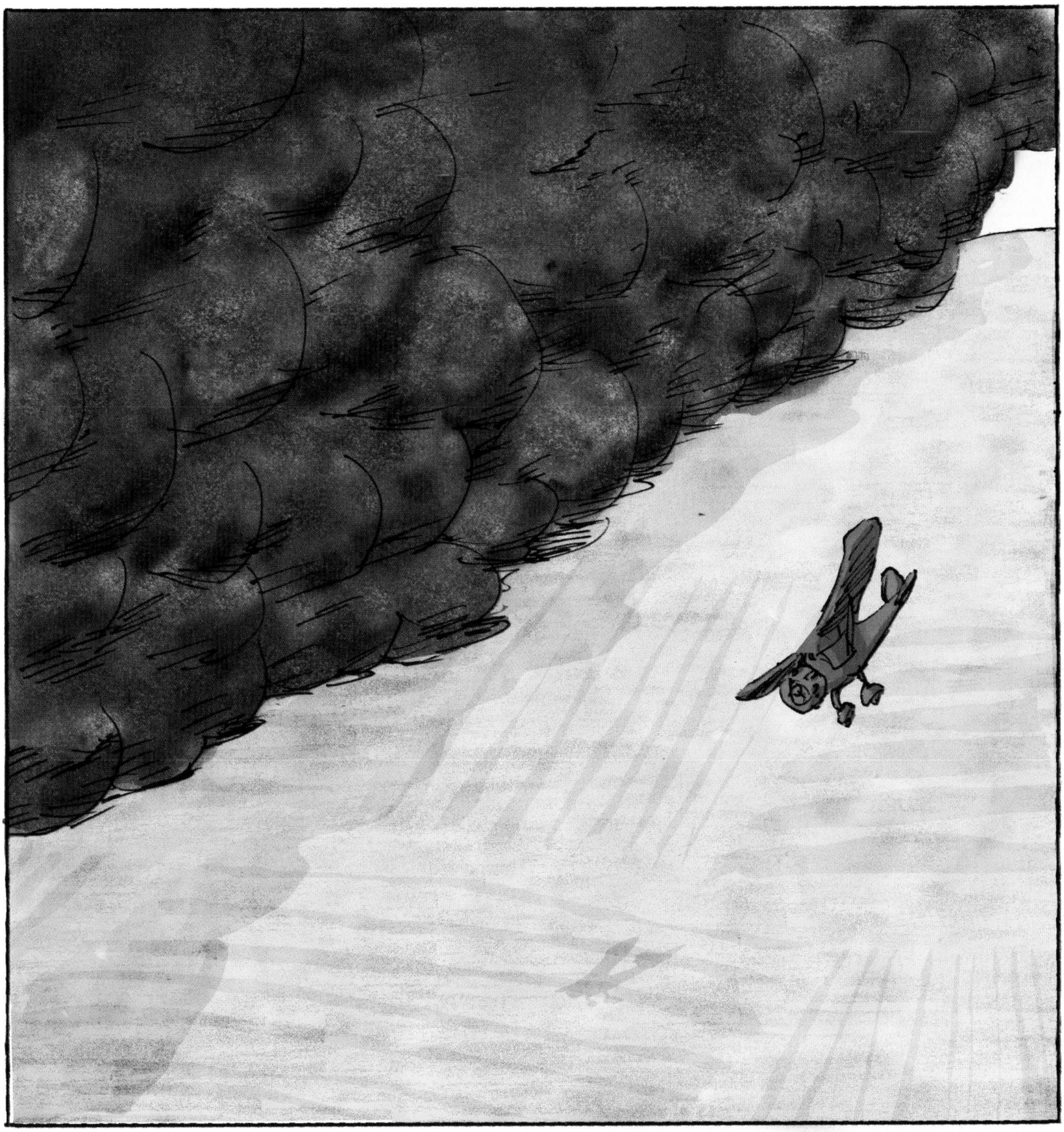

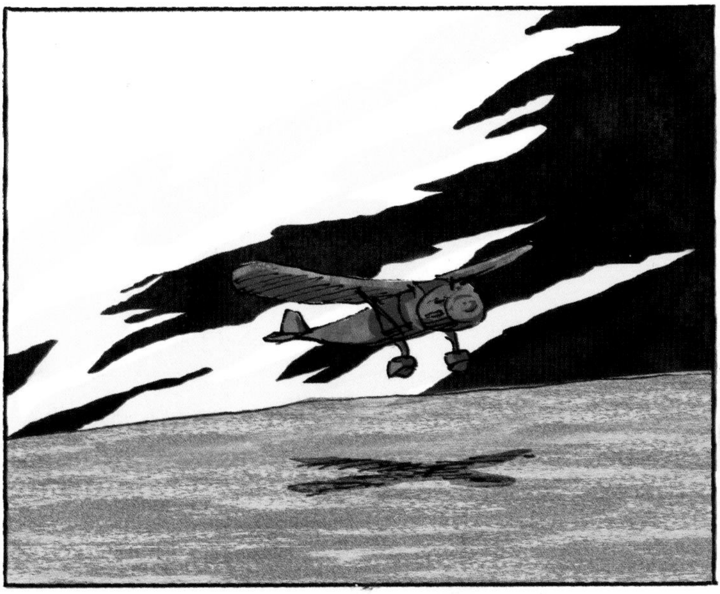

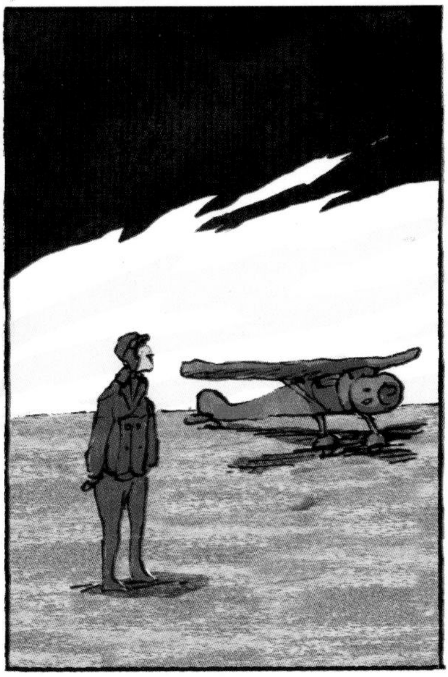

DURING RARE RAINFALLS, MUDDY PELLETS SOMETIMES DROPPED INSTEAD, DENTING CARS AND MAKING COWS BAWL.

WE COULDN'T HAVE A BLIZZARD WITHOUT HAVING DIRT WITH IT. IT LOOKED LIKE CHOCOLATE SNOW.

THE WORST STORMS, BLACK BLIZZARDS, BROUGHT DUST-FILLED DARKNESS.

I TURNED ON A LIGHT AND . . .
ALL YOU COULD SEE WAS BLACK.

PEOPLE LOST THEIR WAY IN THE STORM'S GLOOM, AND SOMETIMES SUFFOCATED TO DEATH.

STORMS COULD BLOW FOR DAYS AND BE IMMEDIATELY

FOLLOWED BY ANOTHER AND ANOTHER, MAKING FOR

RAGING, GRIT-FILLED WINDS SHATTERED WINDOWS AND

TRAINS DERAILED.

UNRELENTING BLOWS FOR WEEKS ON END.

SCOURED THE PAINT OFF HOUSES AND CARS.

TELEPHONE POLES WERE KNOCKED TO THE GROUND.

DEPENDING WHERE IT CAME FROM, THE FLYING DIRT WAS BROWN, BLACK, YELLOW, GRAY, OR RED. SOMETIMES IT WAS AS FINE AS TALC, AND OTHER TIMES, AS COARSE AS GRAVEL. IT COULD TICKLE YOUR NOSE WITH A SHARP, PEPPERY SMELL OR TURN YOUR STOMACH WITH A GREASY STINK.

THE SWIRLING DUST GENERATED STATIC ELECTRICITY. THE AIR FLASHED.

JOLTS OF ELECTRICITY SHOCKED PEOPLE WHEN THEY TOUCHED METAL OR ANOTHER PERSON.

CARS SHORTED OUT AND DIED.

SPIKES ON BARBED-WIRE FENCES GLOWED BLUE.

TONS OF DIRT PER ACRE FELL, PILING UP IN SNOWLIKE DRIFTS.

THE DROUGHT CONTINUED.

ONE YEAR.

TWO YEARS.

THREE YEARS.

DUST GOT INTO EVERYTHING. PEOPLE TAPED THEIR DOORS, STUFFED WALL CRACKS WITH RAGS, AND COVERED WINDOWS WITH SHEETS TO KEEP IT OUT OF THEIR HOUSES. BUT IT STILL SEEPED IN. PEOPLE FANNED THE INSIDE OF THEIR HOUSE WITH WET RAGS TO KEEP THE DUST DOWN. PARENTS SPREAD DAMPENED SHEETS OVER THEIR BABIES' CRIBS.

YOU COULD WRITE YOUR NAME ON THE DIRT OR DUST ON THE TABLE, AND SOMETIMES I'D WIPE THE TABLE OFF TWO OR THREE TIMES BEFORE WE COULD EAT ON IT.

IF YOU WERE COOKING A MEAL, YOU'D END UP WITH DUST IN YOUR FOOD AND YOU WOULD FEEL IT IN YOUR TEETH.

STILL IT SEEPED IN. THE CEILINGS OF SOME HOUSES COLLAPSED FROM THE WEIGHT OF DUST THAT HAD GATHERED IN THE ATTIC.

DUST GOT INTO ANIMALS.

MY HORSE . . . HIS EYES WOULD WATER AND HIS NOSE WOULD WATER, AND I'D WIPE HIS EYES. IT'D JUST BE A LOT OF MUD IN THE PALM OF MY HANDS. I'D DIG IT OUT OF HIS NOSTRILS.

IT BLINDED CHICKENS AND CATTLE, AND CHOKED THEM TO DEATH. SMALL BIRDS AND ANIMALS SUFFOCATED BY THE HUNDREDS IN BAD STORMS.

DUST GOT INTO PEOPLE, TOO.

THE DUST TORE UP THE DELICATE INTERIOR OF THE LUNGS, MAKING PEOPLE SICK AND WEAK. IT BROUGHT CHEST PAINS, SHORTNESS OF BREATH, AND HARD COUGHS THAT COULD BREAK A PERSON'S RIBS. DOCTORS CALLED IT DUST PNEUMONIA. CHILDREN AND THE ELDERLY SUFFERED THE WORST.

THE RED CROSS OPENED SIX EMERGENCY HOSPITALS TO DEAL WITH THE CRISIS. THEY DISTRIBUTED MORE THAN 17,000 DUST MASKS. STILL, HUNDREDS BECAME ILL AND SOME DIED.

ON MAY 9, 1934, WHIRLWINDS LIFTED 350 MILLION TONS OF DIRT FROM THE MONTANA AND THE DAKOTAS' PRAIRIE, GATHERED THEM INTO GRITTY CLOUDS THAT REACHED FIFTEEN THOUSAND FEET, A HEIGHT EQUAL TO TWELVE STACKED EMPIRE STATE BUILDINGS.

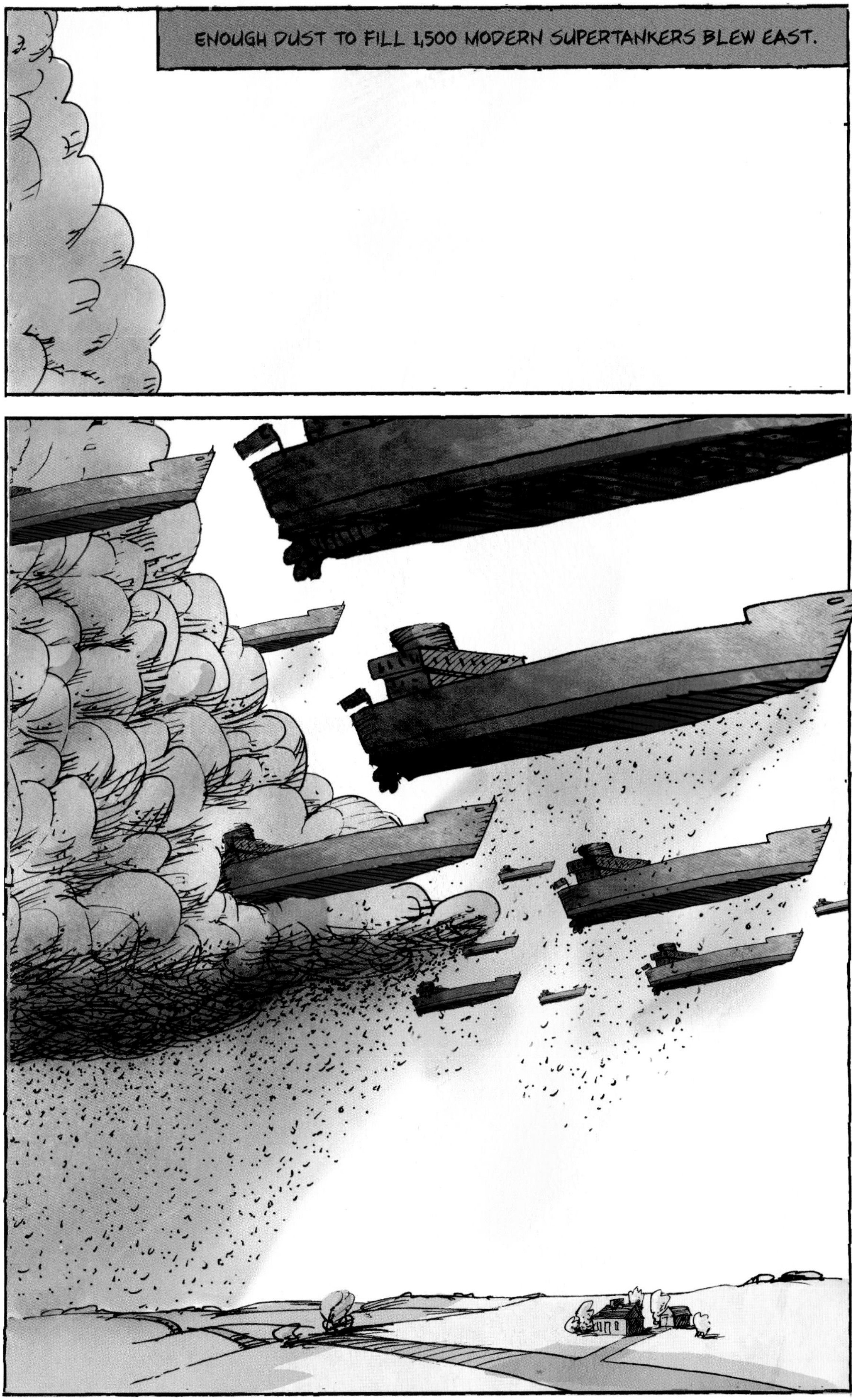
ENOUGH DUST TO FILL 1,500 MODERN SUPERTANKERS BLEW EAST.

DUST FELL LIKE SNOW OVER CHICAGO.

ATLANTA.

BOSTON.

WASHINGTON.

MIDDAY MANHATTAN DARKENED BENEATH A DUSTY GRAY HAZE. CARS SWITCHED ON THEIR HEADLIGHTS TO SEE. THE STATUE OF LIBERTY SEEMED TO DISAPPEAR. EVERYWHERE, DUST: STREETS, SIDEWALKS, GRASS, EVEN THE WATER IN NEW YORK HARBOR.

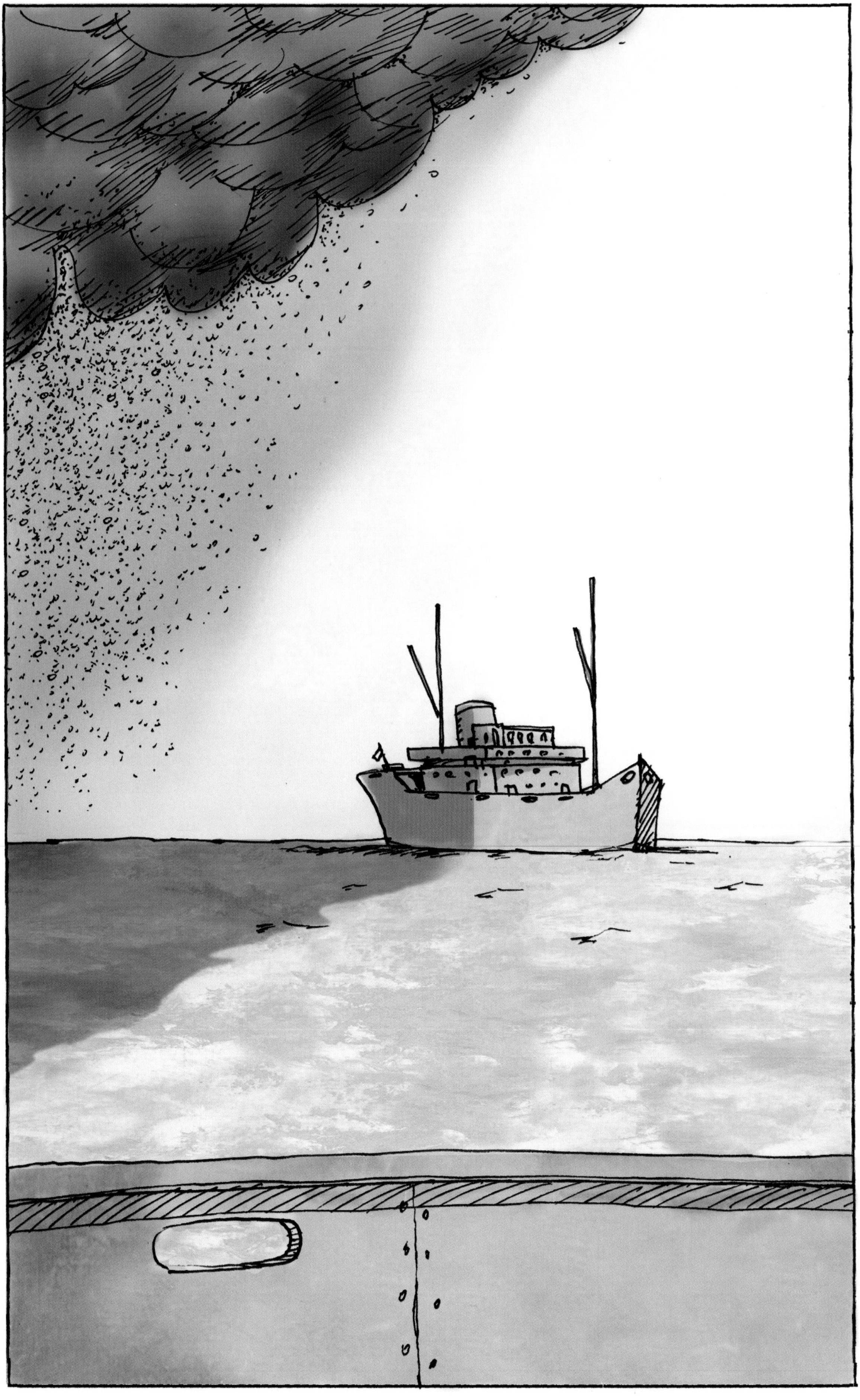

FAR OUT AT SEA, A FINE DIRT GRIT COVERED SHIPS' DECKS
LIKE POWDERED SUGAR ON DOUGHNUTS.

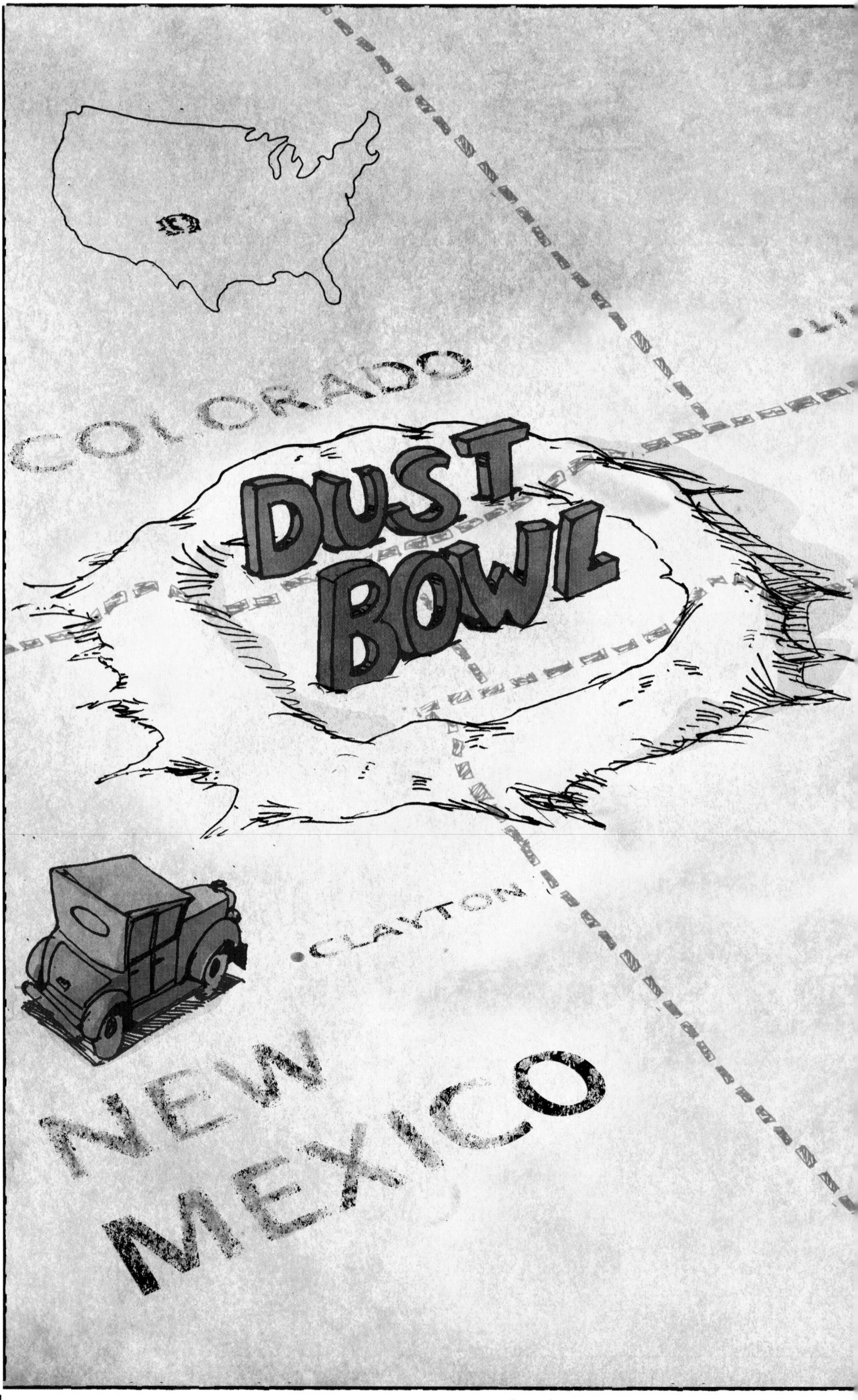
COLORADO
DUST BOWL
CLAYTON
NEW MEXICO

THE WORST OF THE DUSTERS AND BLACK BLIZZARDS WERE FOUND IN A ROUGH CIRCLE COVERING PARTS OF NEW MEXICO, COLORADO, OKLAHOMA, KANSAS, AND TEXAS. THE NEWS REPORTER ROBERT GEIGER CALLED IT THE "DUST BOWL OF THE CONTINENT." THE NAME STUCK.

AND IT WASN'T JUST BLACK BLIZZARDS PLAGUING THE DUST BOWL.

WINTERS WERE COLDER AND SUMMERS HOTTER. SOME PLACES SUF-FERED THEIR COLDEST WINTERS IN FORTY YEARS. SUMMER TEMPERA-TURES TOPPED 100 DEGREES IN OTHERS.

THE WIND WAS LIKE A BLAST FROM A HUGE, RED-HOT FURNACE—CAUSING MY FACE TO BLISTER AND PEEL OFF.

BUGS THAT SHOULD HAVE DIED IN COLDER, WETTER WEATHER OR BEEN EATEN BY BIRDS AND BATS KILLED BY THE DROUGHT NOW TURNED UP EVERYWHERE. CENTIPEDES CRAWLED ACROSS CEILINGS AND WALLS, TARANTULAS MARCHED ACROSS KITCHENS, AND BLACK WIDOW SPIDERS LURKED IN CORNCRIBS AND WOODSHEDS.

THE ANTS WERE SO THICK AND SO BAD THAT YOU COULD SWIPE HANDFULS OF THEM OFF THE TABLE AND STILL HAVE MORE ANTS ON THE TABLE.

MONSTROUS CLOUDS OF MILLIONS OF GRASSHOPPERS APPEARED.

THEY ATE GRASS, TREES, CORN, AND WHEAT, AND WHEN THOSE WERE GONE, THEY TURNED TO FENCE POSTS AND SHOVEL AND RAKE HANDLES.

THEY'D EVEN CHEW A PERSON'S CLOTHES.

THERE WERE GREAT BIG OLD GRASSHOPPERS.

JACKRABBITS RAIDED FIELDS AND GARDENS.

THEY'D EAT THE GRASS OR WHATEVER THERE WAS. WELL, THE LIVESTOCK DIDN'T HAVE ANYTHING. THEY HAD TO GET RID OF THEM.

PEOPLE ORGANIZED RABBIT DRIVES, HERDING THOUSANDS OF THEM INTO PENS AND CLUBBING THEM TO DEATH. AT LEAST THE DEAD RABBITS COULD BE USED FOR FOOD. THE DROUGHT AND DUST STORMS HAD KILLED CROPS AND LIVESTOCK. SOME PEOPLE SURVIVED ON TUMBLEWEED AND ROADKILL.

PEOPLE WERE DESPERATE AND LEAPED TO ANY REMEDY FOR THEIR MISERY, EVEN AN OUTLANDISH ONE. SOMEONE SAID THAT HANGING A DEAD SNAKE FROM A FENCE WOULD BRING RAIN. SOON, FENCES FOR MILES WERE DECORATED WITH DEAD SNAKES.

RAINMAKERS PROMISED THAT THEY COULD COAX WATER FROM THE HEAVENS—FOR A PRICE. THREADBARE TOWNS WORN OUT FROM DROUGHT AND WORN DOWN BY POVERTY SCRAPED MONEY TOGETHER FOR ROCKETS AND KITES TO CARRY DYNAMITE SKYWARD, HOPING TO EXPLODE THE RAIN FROM THE SKY. THEIR PRECIOUS CASH BOUGHT FLASHES AND BOOMS BUT LITTLE ELSE.

WE WATCHED THE WEATHER—WE'D LOOK UP THERE AND SEE A LITTLE CLOUD. OH, WE'D BE SO EXCITED TO SEE IT. OH, I KNOW IT—JUST PRAYED, "COME ON, GIVE US SOME DROPS."

MY YOUTH AND AMBITION WERE GROUND INTO THE VERY DUST ITSELF.

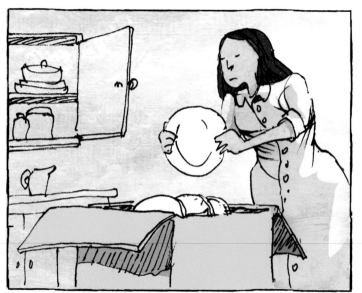

MANY PEOPLE GAVE UP AND LEFT.

SUNDAY, APRIL 14, 1935, THE SOUTHERN PLAINS DAWNED WINDLESS AND "SUN-SHINY." PICNIC WEATHER.

IT WAS A WELCOME CHANGE FROM THE BATTERING FROM FORTY-NINE DUSTERS OF THE PREVIOUS THREE MONTHS. PEOPLE WONDERED IF THE WORST WAS OVER.

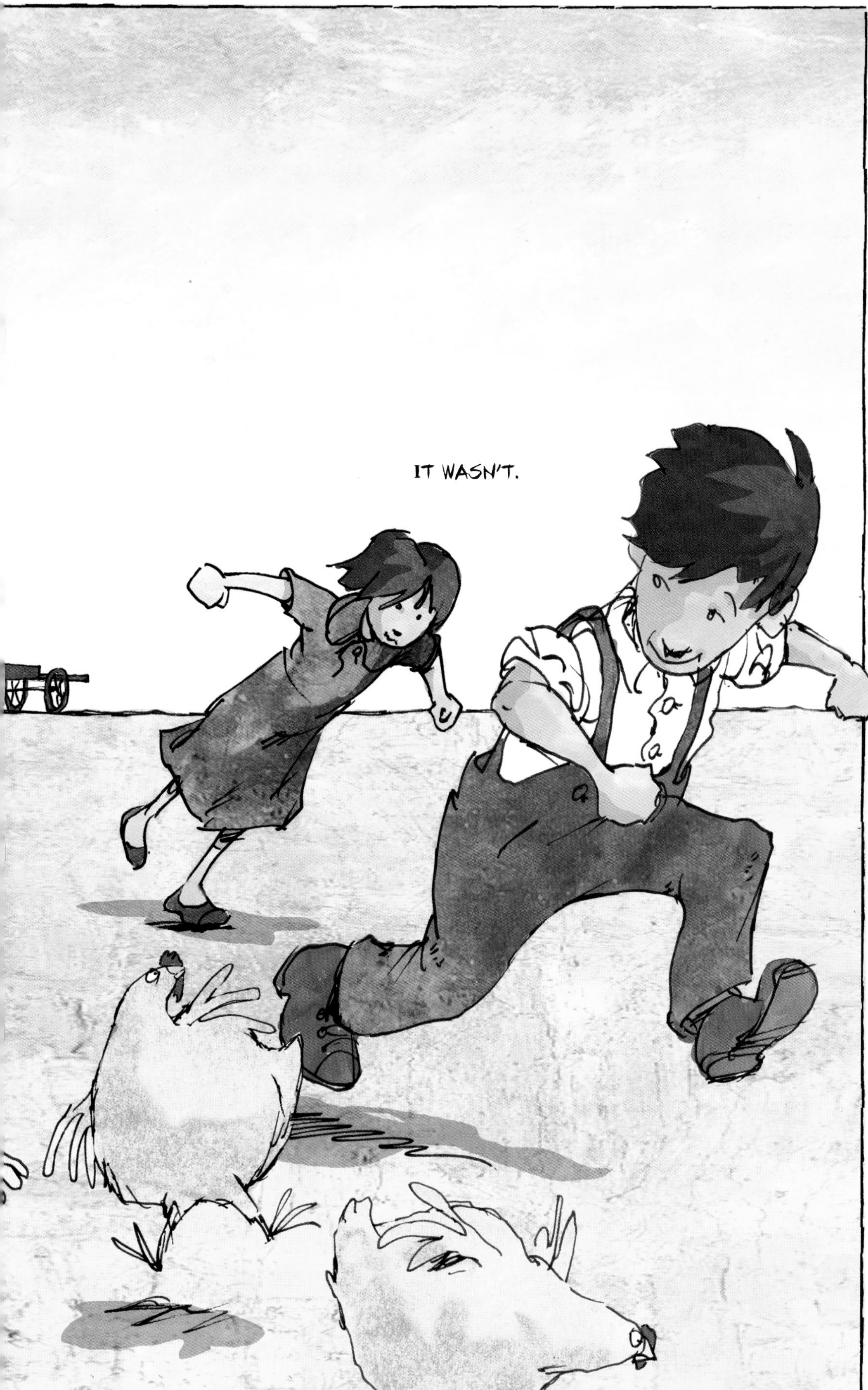
IT WASN'T.

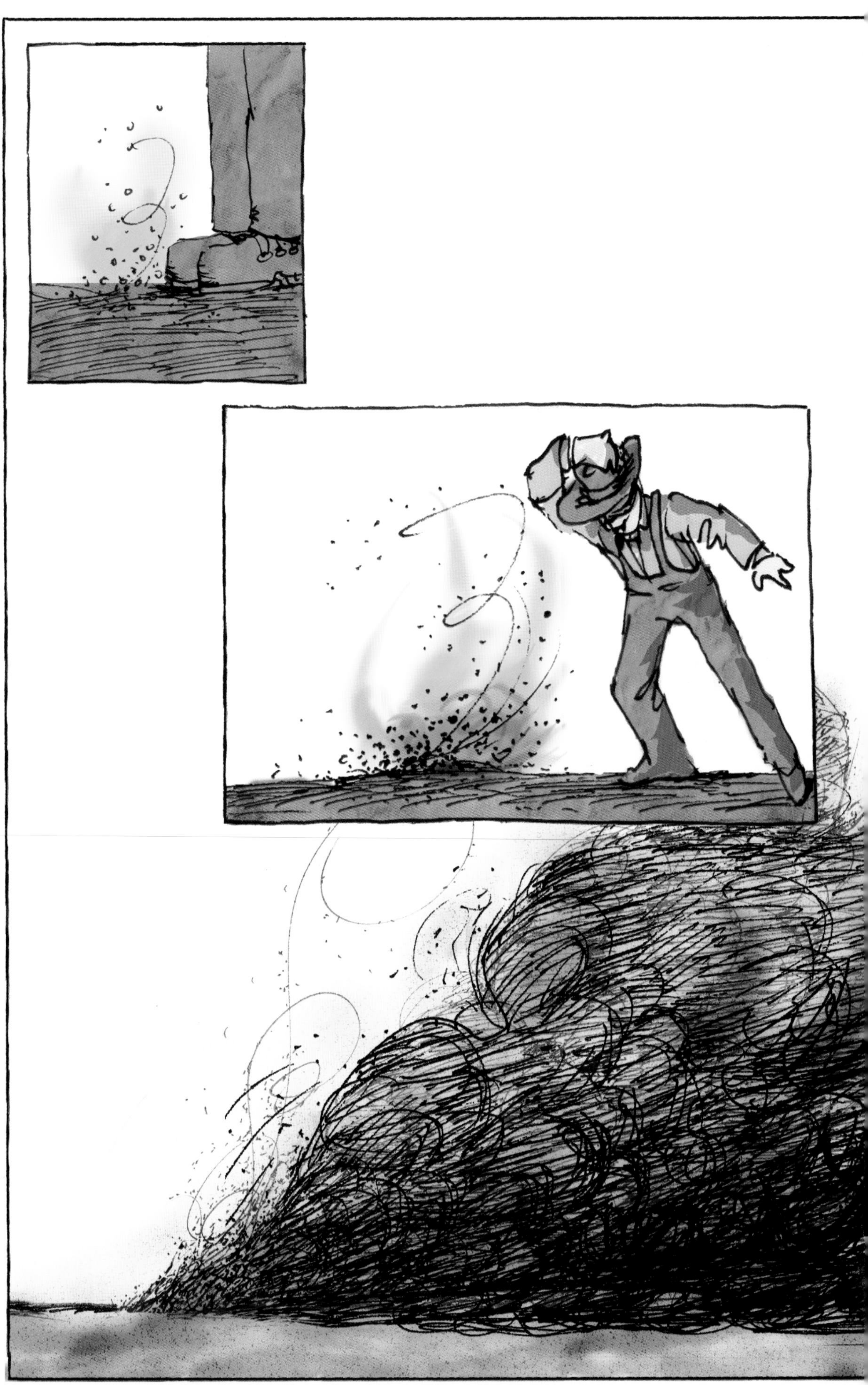

IN WYOMING AND THE DAKOTAS, WILD WINDS— COLD AND STRONG—LIFTED TONS OF DIRT INTO A CHURNING, ROILING, BOILING BLACK CLOUD TWO HUNDRED MILES WIDE.

BIRDS AND JACKRABBITS AND TUMBLEWEEDS ALL RAN IN FRONT OF THE STORM. ELECTRICITY COURSED THROUGH THE AIR, ENOUGH TO POWER NEW YORK CITY.

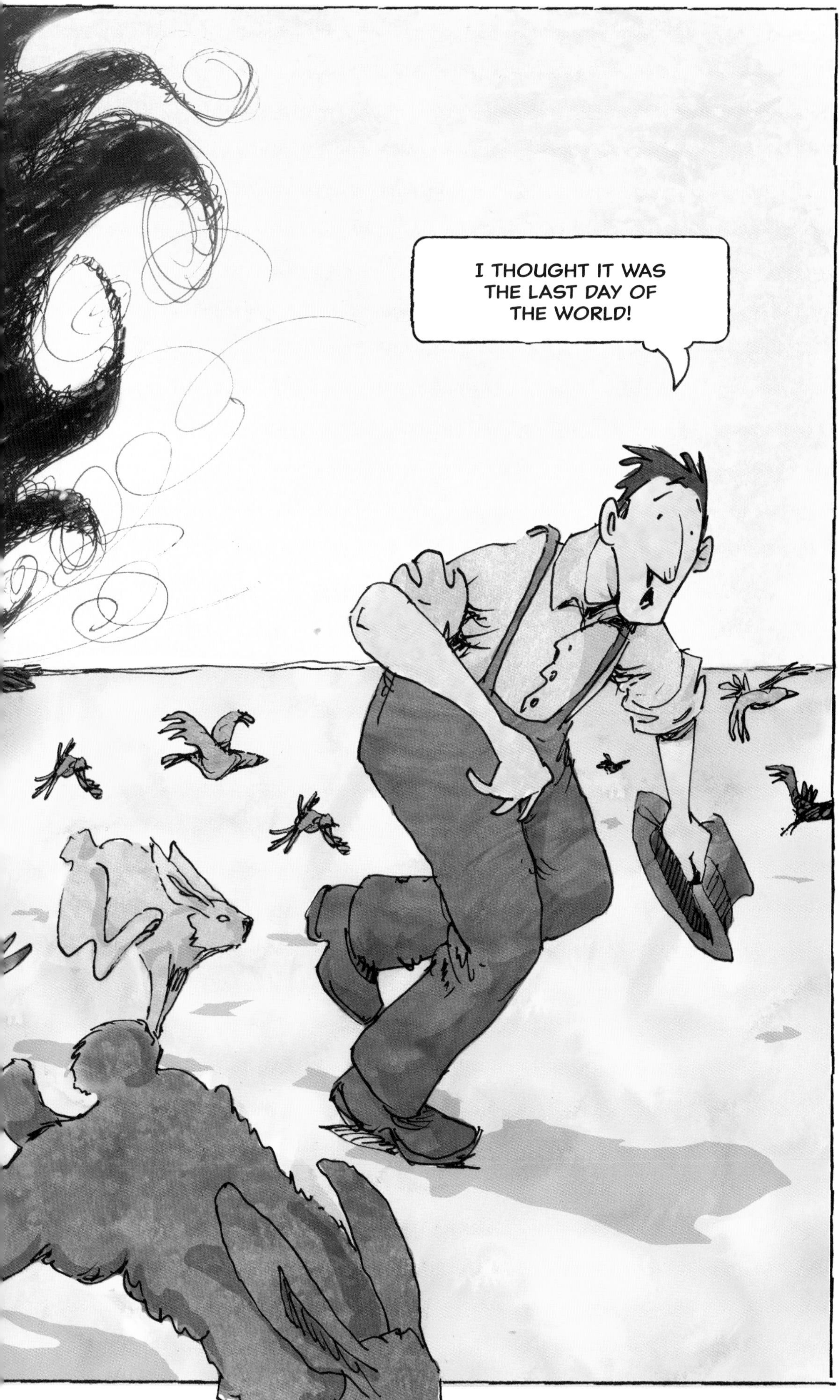
I THOUGHT IT WAS THE LAST DAY OF THE WORLD!

THE TEMPERATURE FELL FIFTY DEGREES. SIXTY-FIVE-MILES-AN-HOUR WINDS AS COARSE AS STEEL WOOL MADE A MONSTROUS CLANKING SOUND.

DRIVERS TRIED OUTRACING IT BUT FAILED.

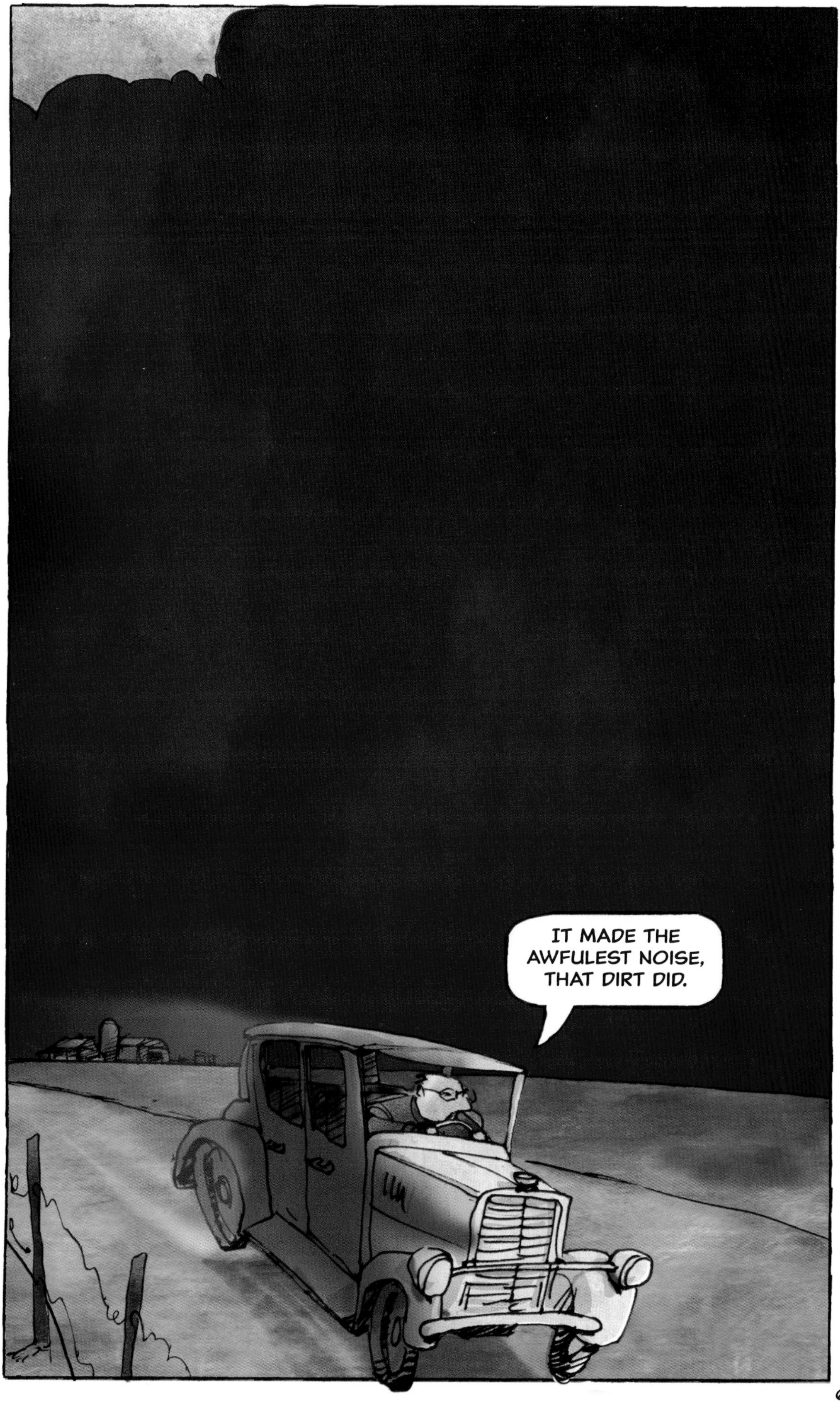
IT MADE THE AWFULEST NOISE, THAT DIRT DID.

PEOPLE CAUGHT IN THE OPEN FELL TO THE GROUND . . .
OR WERE SLAMMED THERE.

DARK, SWIRLING WINDS MADE IT
IMPOSSIBLE TO SEE EVEN THE
HAND IN FRONT OF YOUR FACE.
A BOY PLAYING IN A FIELD DASHED
FOR HIS HOME BUT GOT LOST IN
THE GLOOM. A DRIVER LOST THE
ROAD.

BOTH SUFFOCATED.

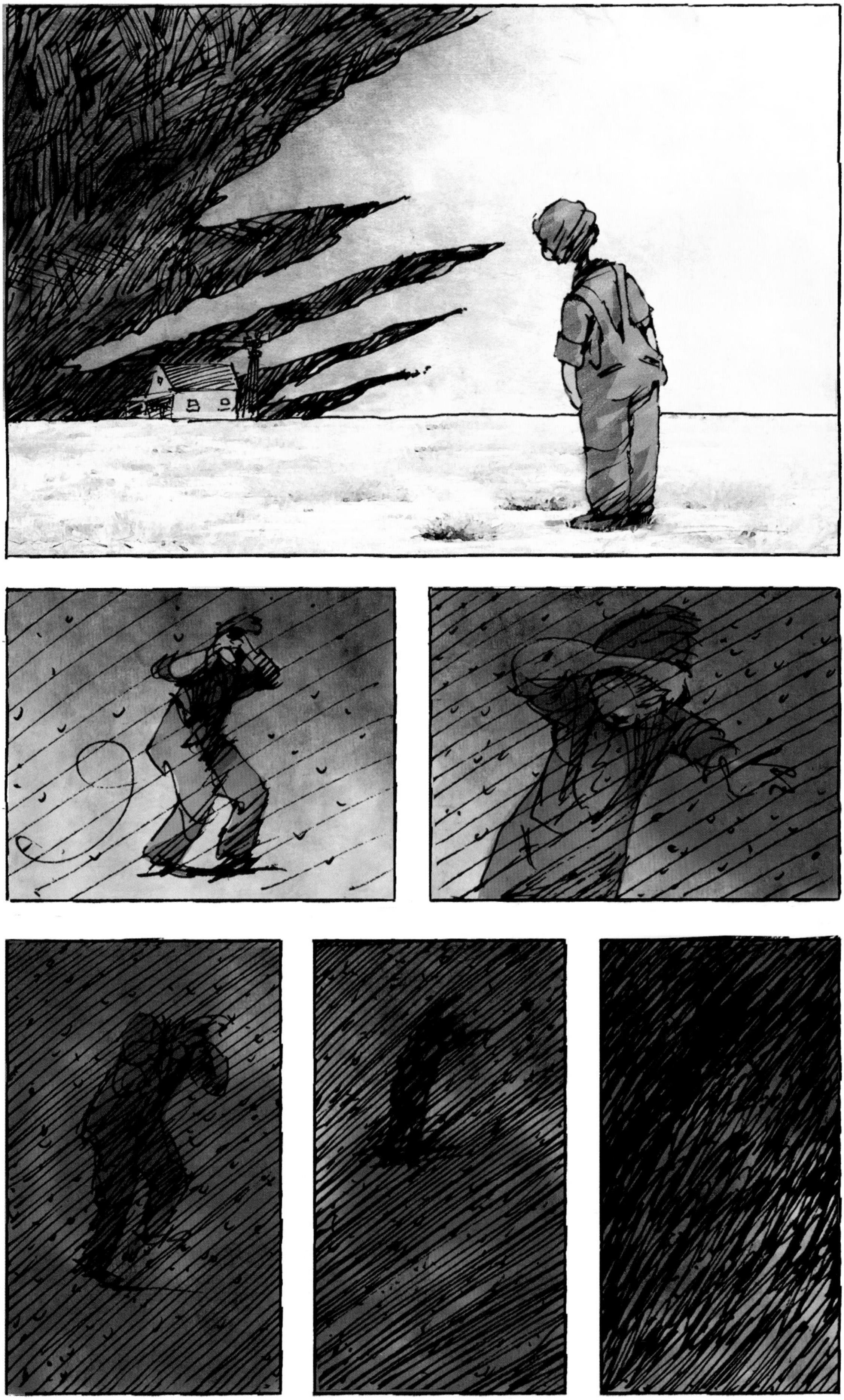

THE REPORTER ROBERT GEIGER AND THE NEWS PHOTOGRAPHER HARRY EISENHARD WERE IN FRONT OF THE BLACK WIND. FROM THEIR STORIES AND PICTURES THE WORLD WOULD LEARN OF THE STORM.

WE WENT DOWN THE ROAD ABOUT SIXTY MILES AN HOUR TO KEEP AHEAD OF IT.

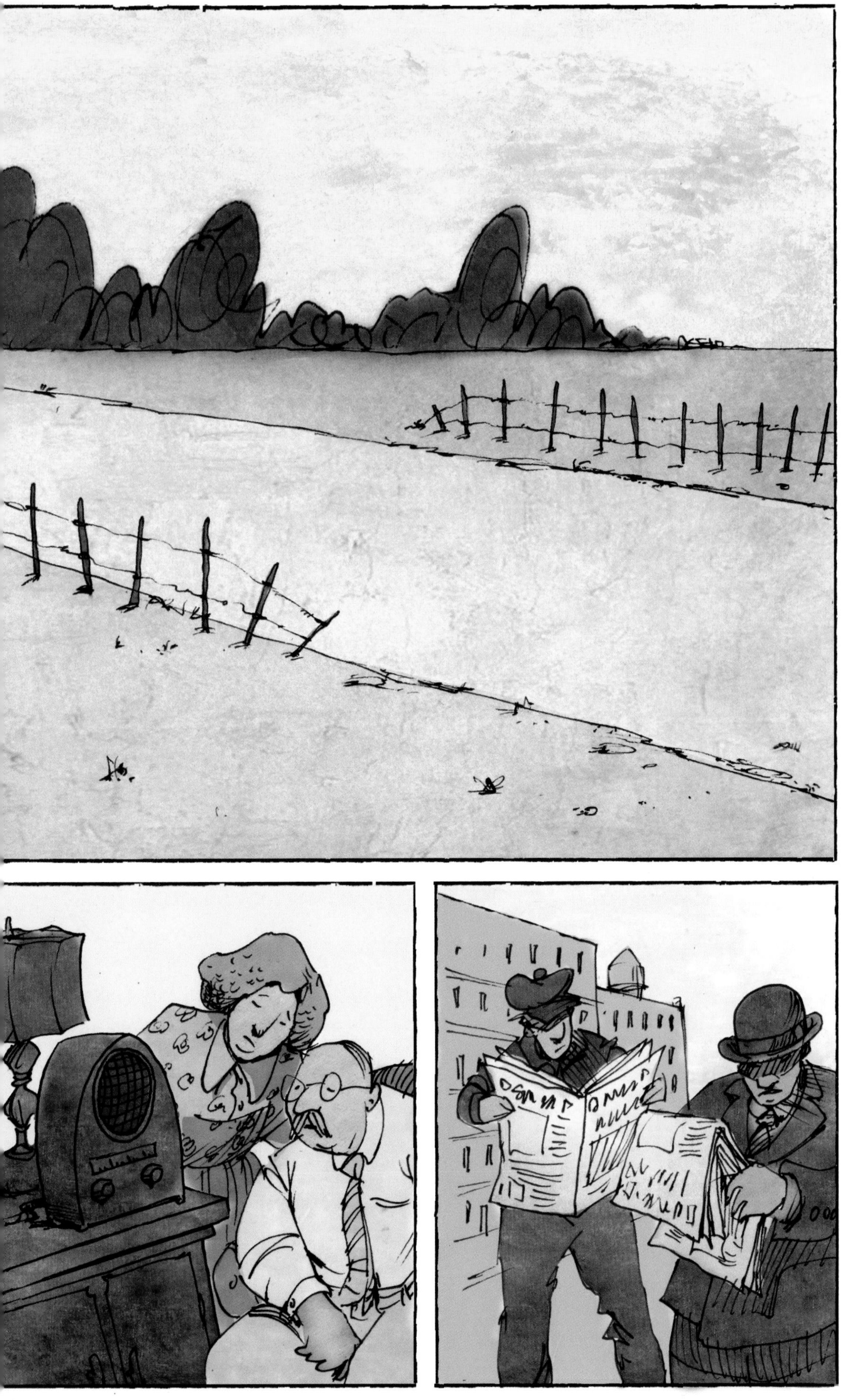

FRIGHTENED PEOPLE RACED FOR SHELTER; HOUSES, BARNS, BASEMENTS, DUGOUTS.

DUST FORCED ITS WAY INTO SHELTERS, DIRTYING THE AIR AND MAKING IT IMPOSSIBLE TO SEE AND DIFFICULT TO BREATHE. THE FOLK SINGER WOODY GUTHRIE HUDDLED IN ONE. HE WOULD LATER BE FAMOUS FOR "THIS LAND IS MY LAND," BUT NOW THE END-OF-THE-WORLD BLACK SUNDAY DUSTER INSPIRED HIM TO WRITE:

"IT FELL ACROSS OUR CITY LIKE A CURTAIN OF BLACK ROLLED DOWN. WE THOUGHT IT WAS OUR . . . DOOM."

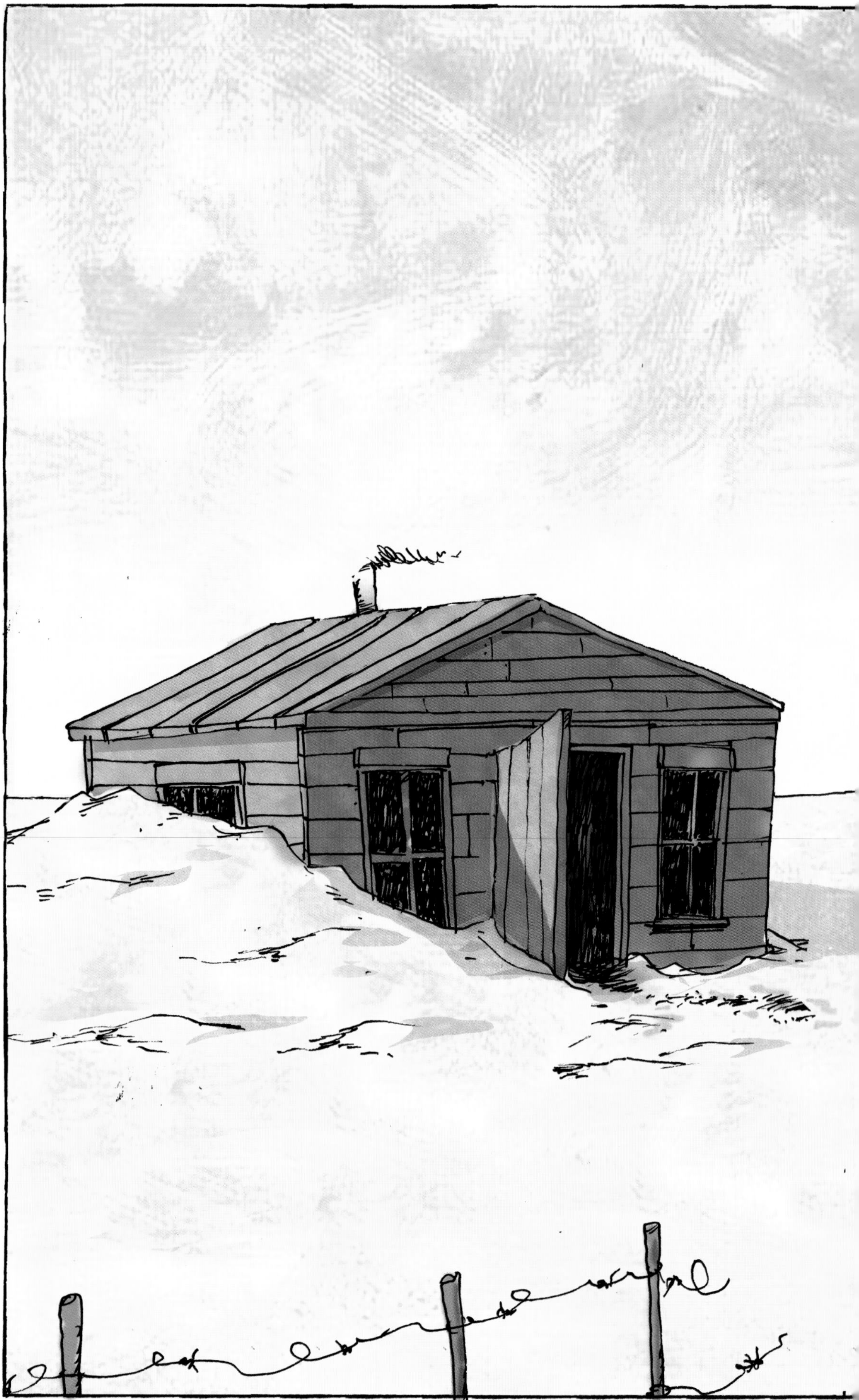

IT WAS THE DUSTER OF A LIFETIME.

AFTER IT GRADUALLY ENDED, PEOPLE DID WHAT THEY DID AFTER EVERY
BLACK BLIZZARD: THEY DUG THE DUST FROM BENEATH THEIR NAILS, WASHED
THEIR FACES, SHOVELED DUST FROM THEIR HOMES, AND STARTED LIFE AGAIN.

PRESIDENT ROOSEVELT AND GOVERNMENT HELPED. THEY PLANTED ABOUT 220 MILLION TREES TO ACT AS WINDBREAKS TO FUTURE DUST STORMS.

THEY BOUGHT MILLIONS ACRES OF LAND TO REPLANT WITH BUFFALO GRASS, THE HARDY GROUND COVER FROM THE TIME OF THE AMERICAN INDIAN.

MOST IMPORTANT, THEY TAUGHT GROWERS TO FARM IN WAYS THAT DIDN'T INJURE THE SOIL.

THE BLACK SUNDAY DUSTER WAS NOT THE END OF DUSTERS OR EVEN THE BEGINNING OF THE END. MORE WOULD FOLLOW. SIXTY-EIGHT IN 1936, SEVENTY-TWO IN 1937, AND ON AND ON UNTIL THE DROUGHT ENDED ABOUT TEN YEARS AFTER IT STARTED.

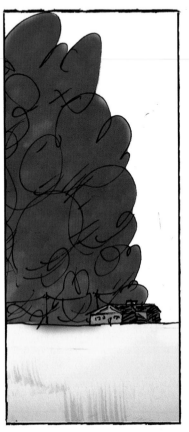

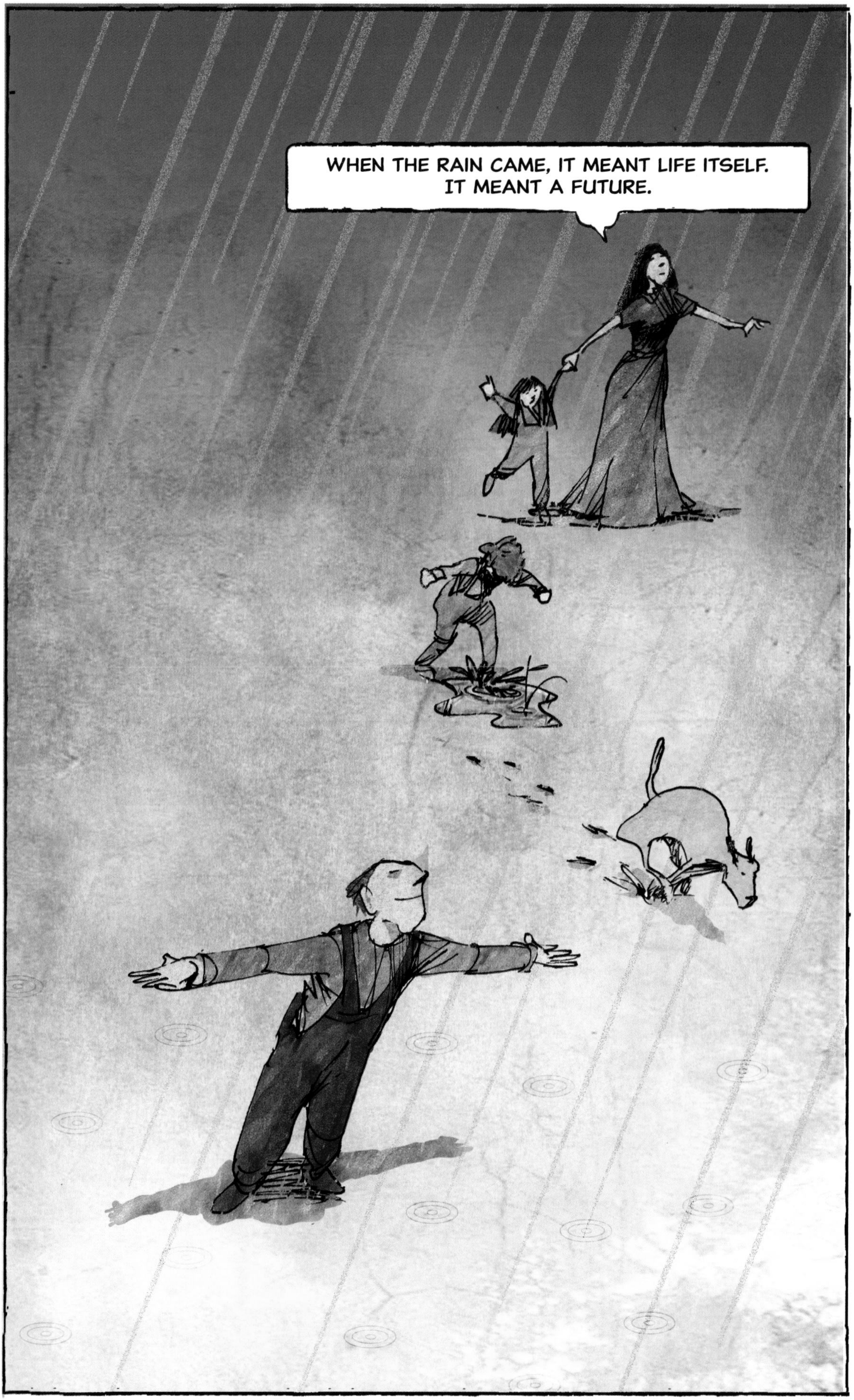
WHEN THE RAIN CAME, IT MEANT LIFE ITSELF. IT MEANT A FUTURE.

AT ITS WORST, ABOUT 100 MILLION ACRES OF TOPSOIL WAS LOST DURING THE DIRTY THIRTIES, AS THE ERA WAS NICKNAMED. ABOUT TWO-THIRDS OF THE ENTIRE GREAT PLAINS WAS DAMAGED BY WIND EROSION. IT HAS STILL NOT COMPLETELY HEALED.

HOW MANY PEOPLE DIED?

HUNDREDS? THOUSANDS? THE RECORDS ARE INACCURATE.

WHATEVER THE GRUESOME ACCOUNTING, IT WAS THE WORST ENVIRONMENTAL CATASTROPHE THE COUNTRY HAS EVER SEEN, AN "UNQUALIFIED DISASTER."

BUT WITH GOVERNMENT HELP AND MORE GRIT THAN ANY BLACK BLIZZARD, DUST BOWLERS REBUILT THEIR LIVES AND REPLANTED THE SOUTHERN PLAINS.

DROUGHT RETURNED IN THE 1950S. AND IN 2011, SCORCHING HEAT CAME BACK AND THE RAIN DISAPPEARED. BOISE CITY, OKLAHOMA, A TOWN RESTING IN THE MIDDLE OF THE OLD DUST BOWL, COUNTED AN UNBROKEN 227 DRY DAYS.

BY 2012, MUCH OF AMERICA WAS UNUSUALLY DRY, AND 55 PERCENT OF THE CONTIGUOUS U.S. SUFFERED MODERATE TO EXTREME DROUGHT.

AND HERE AND THERE ON THE HIGH SOUTHERN PLAIN, SOME VETERANS OF THE 1930S DUSTERS REMAIN, THEIR NUMBERS DWINDLING, STILL KEEPING A FINGER TO THE WIND AND EYE OUT FOR RAIN.

SELECTED BIBLIOGRAPHY

Bonnifield, Paul. *The Dust Bowl: Men, Dirt, and Depression.* Albuquerque: University of New Mexico Press, 1979.

Egan, Timothy. *The Worst Hard Time.* Boston: Houghton Mifflin, 2006.

Encyclopedia Britannica Online, s.v. "Plains Indian." Accessed October 25, 2012, www.britannica.com/EBchecked/topic/462761/Plains-Indian.

Hurt, Douglas R. *The Dust Bowl: An Agricultural and Social History.* Chicago: Nelson-Hall, 1981.

Levy, Matthys, and Mario Salvadori. *Why the Earth Quakes.* New York: W. W. Norton, 1995.

NOAA-NWS website glossary, s.v. "dry thunderstorm." Accessed October 25, 2012, www.weather.gov/glossary/index.php?word=dry+thunderstorm.

Oklahoma Oral History Research Project. *Dust, Drought and Dreams Gone Dry: Oklahoma Women and the Dust Bowl.* Special Collections and University Archives, Edmon Low Library, Oklahoma State University, 2001.

Surviving the Dust Bowl. Transcript. PBS's American Experience series, www.pbs.org/wgbh/americanexperience/dustbowl.

Worster, Donald. *Dust Bowl: The Southern Plains in the 1930s.* New York: Oxford University Press, 1979.

Wunder, John R., editor, et al. *Americans View Their Dust Bowl Experience.* Niwot: University Press of Colorado, 1999.

Dust storm threatens Stratford, Texas, in 1935.

SOURCE NOTES

"Oh my God": Egan, 204.

On a clear, warm Sunday: Worster, 18-20; Hunt, 42; Egan, 198.

Panicked birds: Hurt, 2.

The temperature: Worster, 18.

Electricity coursed: Egan, 204.

Frightened people: Egan, 204.

Sixty to one hundred million years: Worster, 67.

The Rockies were born: Levy, 23-27; Worster, 67.

To the east: Worster, 69.

And the plain behind: Hurt, 16-19; Egan, 25.

About half: www.esrl.noaa.gov/psd/data/usclimate/pcp.state.19712000.climo;
       www.sercc.com/climateinfo_files/monthly/Georgia_prcp.html.

It's too little: Worster, 71-72.

American Indians: Worster, 77; Encyclopedia Brittanica.

Pioneers from the settled: Worster, 77; Egan, 21.

Ranchers were sure: Egan, 19.

In the southern plains: Egan, 21-22.

The ranchers' hard luck: Egan, 24.

Farmers bought: Egan, 37.

"It was nothing": OOHRP pdf 2819.

"There wasn't": OOHRP pdf 2819.

Despite their sweat: Egan, 42.

A hungry world: Egan, 42.

Seeing the profit: Worster, 89.

Plowing all those acres: Worster, 90-91; Hurt, 23.

A tractor took: Egan, 47.

Suddenly farmers enjoyed: Egan, 44.

Then the war ended: Hurt, 31; Egan, 79, 86.

"It was like somebody": OOHRP pdf 2831.

In 1931: Worster, 11.

The drought tortured: Worster, 12-13; Egan, 112.

In January 1932: Hurt, 33.

Fourteen more dusters: Worster, 15.

"A terrible dust storm": OOHRP pdf 2813.

One duster trapped: Egan, 139; Hurt, 34.

During rare rainfalls: Egan, 139.

"We couldn't have a blizzard": OOHRP pdf 2816.

The worst storms: Worster, 15.

"I turned on a light": OOHRP pdf 2891.

Storms could blow for days: Egan, 194, 173; Worster, 15; Hurt, 42.

Raging, grit-filled: Egan, 122, 138-39.

Telephone poles: Egan, 167, 175; Hurt, 38, 40; Worster, 16.

Depending where it came: Egan, 185; Worster, 15.

The swirling dust: Egan, 204-6, 211-19.

Tons of dirt: Egan, 188.

The drought continued: Egan, 153.

People fanned the inside: OOHRP pdf 2843, pdf 2819.

"It's lighter than air": OOHRP pdf 2891.

"You could write": OOHRP pdf 2843.

"If you were cooking": Surviving transcript, 5.

The ceilings of some: Hurt, 39.

"My horse": OOHRP pdf 2849.

It blinded chickens: Worster, 22.

The dust tore up: Egan, 173-74, 180; Worster, 20.

The Red Cross: Hurt, 52.

On May 9, 1934 to Far out at sea: Worster, 13; Egan, 151-52.

The worst of the dusters: Worster, 28-30.

Winters were colder and summers: Egan, 117, 174; Worster, 12.

"The wind was like": Surviving transcript, 17.

Bugs that should have died: Egan, 115.

"The ants were so thick": OOHRP pdf 2849.

They ate grass, trees, corn: Egan, 284.

"There were great big": OOHRP pdf 2828.

"The'd eat the grass": OOHRP pdf 2849.

People organized rabbit drives: Hurt, 50, 205; Egan, 117, 141, 163, 165.

People were desperate: Egan, 190.

Rainmakers promised: Egan, 231; Hurt, 53-54.

"We watched the weather": OOHRP pdf 2864.

"My youth and ambition": Surviving transcript, 20.

Sunday, April 14, 1935: Worster, 18; OOHRP pdf 2882.

In Wyoming and the Dakotas: Egan, 203; OOHRP pdf 2849; Hurt, 1-2.

Electricity coursed through: Egan, 221.

"I thought it": OOHRP pdf 2882.

The temperature fell: Worster, 18; Egan, 206.

Drivers tried outracing: Egan, 204.

"It made the awfulest": OOHRP pdf 2849.

People caught: Egan, 206, 211.

Dark, swirling winds: Egan, 210, 219.

A boy playing: Egan, 203; Surviving transcript, 11.

The reporter Robert Geiger: Egan, 203.

"We went down the road": www.perryton.com/black.htm.

Frightened people raced: Egan, 204, 211.

Dust forced its way into shelters: Egan, 220; Worster, 9.

President Roosevelt and government: Egan, 309-11.

The Black Sunday duster: Worster, 17; Surviving transcript, 20.

"When the rain came": Surviving transcript, 21.

At its worst: Egan, 223-24, 304.

Boise City, Oklahoma: www.huffingtonpost.com/2011/05/10/texas-drought-2011-record_n_859902.html.

Monster dust storm sweeps over Phoenix, Arizona, in 2011.